THE *Cat Burglar* OF PETHAVEN DRIVE

Written by Sally Farrell Odgers
Illustrated by Mary Davy

00 99 98 97 96

10 9 8 7 6 5 4 3 2

Published by Shortland Publications Limited, 2B Cawley St, Ellerslie, Auckland, New Zealand.

Distributed in the United States of America by

a division of Reed Elsevier Inc.
500 Coventry Lane
Crystal Lake, IL 60014
800-822-8661

Distributed in Canada by

PRENTICE HALL GINN
1870 Birchmount Road
Scarborough
Ontario M1P 2J7

Printed through Bookbuilders Limited, Hong Kong

ISBN: 0-7901-0982-4

WRITTEN BY SALLY FARRELL ODGERS ILLUSTRATED BY MARY DAVY

REMOVAL
Company
SOLD
RM 145

It all started when The Walking Dogfight left town.

Hallelujah! OwOOOOOO!

Excuse me – that was just yours truly giving a howl of thanksgiving. Until quite recently, The Walking Dogfight lived at Number 1 Pethaven Drive, two doors down from me. The Walking Dogfight was as ugly as sin with a temper to match.

Now, I always try to look on the bright side. You just ask The Kids and my Missus. "Good old Mr. D," they'll tell you. "Always looks on the bright side. What a wonderful dog he is!" I never found any bright side to The Walking Dogfight. I don't think he had one.

But let's get on with the story.

I sat watching while his kennel was loaded into the moving van. The Walking Dogfight was bundled in after it and I gave him a great send-off. After all, he *was* my worst enemy.

"Hallelujah! OwOOOOOO!"

The Walking Dogfight gave me a last dirty look, then the doors banged shut. And that was that.

“That’s that, then,” I said. “All my troubles are over!”

“Oh, *are* they?” said a sly, cattish sort of voice. “Are they really?”

I turned around, and there was my second worst enemy, The Mean Monstrosity, gloating on a gatepost.

“So now there’s just the two of us,” continued The Mean Monstrosity. “Right, Mr. D?”

I gazed at the sky. "I think it's going to rain," I said. "I'm sure it's going to rain. In bucketfuls. *Right... now!*"

Swofffffft!

That was The Mean Monstrosity running for cover. If there's one thing that cat cannot abide, it's rain.

He got back at me, of course. First, he ignored me for three hours, then he shot around the corner of his house yowling "Eeyowfffttzz!" at the top of his lungs.

Now any dog who calls himself a dog will chase a howling cat, so I shot around the corner after him. Slap, bang, ouch into a cactus.

There's never been a cactus there before, so I reckoned The Mean Monstrosity's Missus must have planted it that very day. Anyway, I ran into it at full speed.

"OwOOOOOO!" This time it *wasn't* a howl of thanksgiving.

MR D

I rushed in through the dog flap and whined for help. "Poor Mr. D," said The Kids. "He's got a prickle in his nose." They took it out with tweezers, and slapped on a big bandage. It took ages before they got it to stick, so I was late getting out to my dinner. Can you suppose what I found?

Yes, I found The Mean Monstrosity crouched over *my* bowl, crunching up the last of *my* Doggities.

"That does it!" I said. "From now on, it's war!" And it was.

Did I drop off for a snooze under my favorite bush?

The Mean Monstrosity would spring an ambush and terrorize my tail.

Did I close my eyes for even half a second at feeding time?

The Mean Monstrosity would leap from nowhere and dine on my dinner. Or sometimes he'd do something worse to my dinner. He'd... but no, it's too disgusting to mention.

Some of the things he did to me that week shouldn't happen to a cat – let alone a poor defenseless dog like me.

Then a moving van arrived at Number 1.

Oh no! I thought. The Walking Dogfight! He's back! And I ran to hide in the coat closet.

Every creak made me think The Walking Dogfight was pushing open the gate.

Every draft made me think The Walking Dogfight was breathing down my neck.

In the end, I came out of the closet and slunk out of the dog flap. If The Walking Dogfight was back, *I* was leaving town.

Guess who was waiting outside?

Well, it wasn't The Walking Dogfight and it wasn't The Mean Monstrosity. It was another cat.

“Hallelujah! OwOOOOOO!” That was me giving another howl of thanksgiving.

He was the longest, narrowest cat I’d ever seen. Let me put it this way. Have you ever seen a dachshund? Well, double the length and halve the depth, and you’ll get the right idea.

He was a sort of gym-sock gray, with eyes the color of ripe bananas. He was washing his ears with one front paw. And, as he didn’t spit in my eye or terrorize my tail, I could tell at a glance he was my kind of cat.

"Hi," I said. "Do you steal Doggities?"

The cat considered. "No," he said. "Never touch the things." And he went on washing. "What's your name?" he asked through a mouthful of paw.

"They call me Mr. D," I said. "Who are you?"

The cat had hoisted one hind leg in the air, now he peered underneath and spat out a few gray hairs. "They call me Sylvester Slink. I've just moved into Number 1. Now, you know the neighborhood. Who's Public Enemy Number One?"

I must have looked blank, because he spat out some more hairs and explained. "There's a villain in every neighborhood. Sometimes it's a cat-chasing dog. Sometimes it's a cat-hating man. Sometimes it's a cat-calling cockatoo. Who is it here?"

"Well," I said, "I suppose it's The Mean Monstrosity. He's a very ugly cat at Number 2 and he's trouble. Always."

Sylvester Slink nodded two or three times. "Thank you for that information," he said. "I'll be sure to remember that." And he slid away.

MR. D

That night, while I was snoozing in the kitchen, I heard a scuffling sound. I looked up and saw a chicken sliding through the dog flap.

That's right. A chicken.

Let me explain. It wasn't alive. It was the sort of chicken my Missus stuffs with bread crumbs and onions and bakes in the oven. Until five minutes ago, this chicken had been thawing in the fridge. Now it was halfway out of the dog flap. Any dog who calls himself a dog must alert the family to vanishing chickens, so I launched into my most deep-throated, threatening *woo-woo-woof* and woke The Family.

"Be quiet, Mr. D!" yelled my Missus.

I know my duty, so I *woo-woo-woofed* again and out they came.

"I said, be quiet, Mr. D!" yelled my Missus. Then she spotted the chicken caught by one drumstick in the hinge of the dog flap. "Well, will you look at that!" she said. "We've been burglarized!" She opened the door and leaned out. Of course, she couldn't see anything, but later I heard a small, cattish snigger from outside in the dark. This time, The Mean Monstrosity had gone *too* far.

In the morning, Sylvester Slink was in my yard, washing his chest. Bob, bob, bob went his head. I said, "That Mean Monstrosity came into my kitchen last night and stole The Family's Sunday dinner."

"That's too bad." Sylvester Slink spat out some hairs. "What are you going to do?"

“Do? I’m going to have it out with him!” I said.

I put my eye to the big knothole in the fence between my garden and The Mean Monstrosity’s. The Mean Monstrosity’s eye was looking back.

“I’ll get you for this!” I said.

The next night, there was a commotion at Number 4. In the morning, Missus Number 4 came to complain to *my* Missus.

"It's my old rooster!" said Missus Number 4. "That dreadful cat's been after my old rooster! All his tail feathers! Gone!"

While my Missus gave Missus Number 4 some coffee, I looked at Old Rooster. He certainly did look bald around the bottom. "Who did it?" I asked.

"A cat, an ugly cat with evil eyes!" yelled Old Rooster. "That's who doodle-doodle-did it!"

Just as I'd expected. I went home and found Sylvester Slink washing his tail in my yard. "The Mean Monstrosity has struck again," I said. "He's taken up cat burglary."

"Tch, tch," went Sylvester Slink, inspecting his tail. "Cats like him give the whole tribe a bad name."

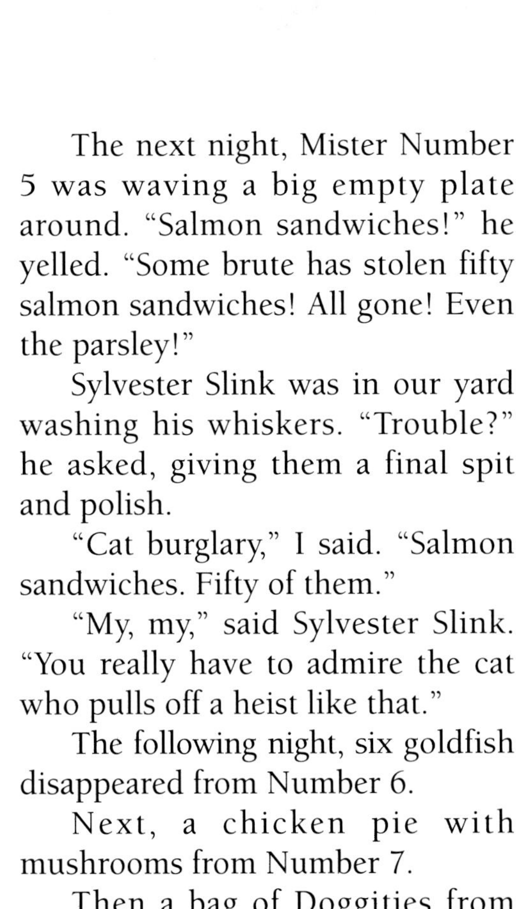

The next night, Mister Number 5 was waving a big empty plate around. "Salmon sandwiches!" he yelled. "Some brute has stolen fifty salmon sandwiches! All gone! Even the parsley!"

Sylvester Slink was in our yard washing his whiskers. "Trouble?" he asked, giving them a final spit and polish.

"Cat burglary," I said. "Salmon sandwiches. Fifty of them."

"My, my," said Sylvester Slink. "You really have to admire the cat who pulls off a heist like that."

The following night, six goldfish disappeared from Number 6.

Next, a chicken pie with mushrooms from Number 7.

Then a bag of Doggities from Number 8.

"Strange thing for a cat to take," said Sylvester Slink when I told him the news.

"Not at all," I snapped. "The Mean Monstrosity *loves* Doggities."

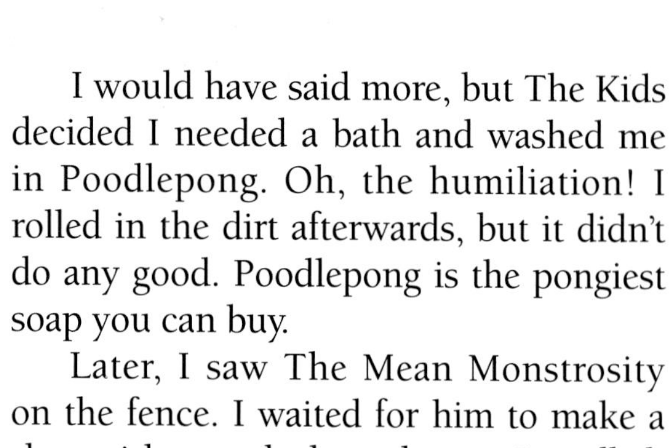

I would have said more, but The Kids decided I needed a bath and washed me in Poodlepong. Oh, the humiliation! I rolled in the dirt afterwards, but it didn't do any good. Poodlepong is the pongiest soap you can buy.

Later, I saw The Mean Monstrosity on the fence. I waited for him to make a sly, cattish remark about the way I smelled. I waited for him to boast about his career in cat burglary. Not a word. His tail was down and his whiskers looked worried.

"Hey, Kitsyboy!" I said. "How's Mommy's Diddums this morning?" That always gets him going, but not this time. I nipped his tail, just to see if he was alive. "What's up?" I asked. "Cat got your tongue? Too full to speak? I mean, fifty sandwiches? Six goldfish? A whole packet of Doggities? That's going too far, even for you."

The Mean Monstrosity glowered at me. "I've been framed!" he spat. "Everything's being cat burgled and everyone's blaming me and *I didn't do it*."

That was such a good joke I told it to Sylvester Slink on my way home.

The next night, a stuffed pilchard was pilfered from Number 9. Next, a tub of butter and some imported cheese vanished from Number 10.

"That cat," said my Missus, "has gone too far." And she stamped over to Number 2. I followed to

hear the fun. “If he keeps this up,” said my Missus, “he’ll be sent to the pound.”

Hallelujah! OwOOOOOO!

That was me, giving a howl of thanksgiving at the thought.

Over the next two days, I didn't see The Mean Monstrosity at all. And an odd thing happened. Now that my enemy had stopped persecuting me, life seemed to have lost its savor. It just wasn't the same without those flying claws and rude remarks. Even my Doggities didn't taste right now that I could eat them in peace. Plus, I couldn't help thinking about the pound. And though I hate The Mean Monstrosity, he *is* my second worst enemy, and if a dog can't give his second worst enemy a bit of advice, he has no right to call himself a dog.

So, on Friday morning, I squeezed under The Mean Monstrosity's gate. "Hey, Kitsyboy!" I hissed. "Joke's over, OK?"

I was shocked at the way he looked. *Really* downtrodden. "What do *you* want?" he asked.

"I want you to stop this cat burglary," I said. "You'll get put in the pound, and you know what *that* means."

The Mean Monstrosity shuddered. He knew what that meant, all right.

"WeOWWWW!" That was The Mean Monstrosity giving a yowl of dismay. "I can't stop it, you demented dog!" he squealed. "Know why? It isn't me that's doing it! I *told* you that."

This time I believed him. And I made a brilliant deduction. "If it isn't you," I said, "it must be someone else."

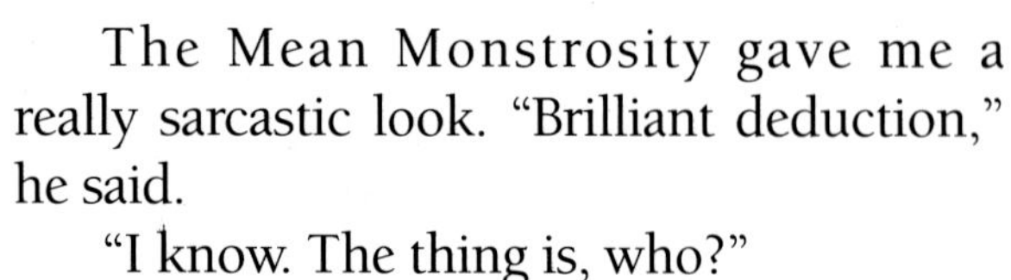

The Mean Monstrosity gave me a really sarcastic look. "Brilliant deduction," he said.

"I know. The thing is, who?"

"That new cat," growled The Mean Monstrosity. "Who else?"

"Sylvester Slink?" I said. "It can't be. He doesn't like Doggities. There's only one cat around here who likes Doggities, and that's you."

"And how do you know he doesn't like Doggities?"

"He told me."

"And does he know I like Doggities?" asked The Mean Monstrosity.

"How could he..." I began, then I stopped. "Well yes," I admitted. "I'm afraid he does. I told him."

"Traitor," said The Mean Monstrosity. "Now listen here, Mr. D. You tell that cat anything else about me, and you're *history*."

"I think it's going to rain," I said. "I'm *sure* it's going to rain. In bucketfuls. Right... *now*!"

Swoffffft!

That was The Mean Monstrosity running for cover. As I said, he cannot *abide* rain.

I went over to Number 1. There was Sylvester Slink, washing his paws. "Hello, there," he said. "What did that wicked cat burglar burgle last night?"

I opened my mouth to call him a thief, then I had another brilliant idea. "I think it's going to rain," I said. "I'm *sure* it's going to rain. In bucketfuls. Right... *now*!"

Hhhhfff. Flooomp.

That was Sylvester Slink yawning and flopping over on the path to rest.

"I *said*," I repeated, "I think it's going to rain. I'm sure it's going to rain. In bucketfuls. Right... *now*!"

"So?" yawned Sylvester Slink. "I don't mind rain. It saves on the washing."

"Aha!" I said, and went home.

MR. D

The Mean Monstrosity was waiting for me. "I'll get you for that, Mr. D," said The Mean Monstrosity. "It didn't rain at all."

"That's right," I said. "But you'd better hope it rains soon."

The Mean Monstrosity spat in my eye.

"If you're going to take it *that* way, Kitsyboy," I said, "I *won't* help you after all."

That got his attention, so I told him my plan.

"You're sure I don't have to get wet?" he said anxiously.

"Quite sure, Kitsyboy," I said. "In fact, the whole plan *depends* on you *not* getting wet. Another thing – stay with your Missus all night. Sit on her knee. Sleep on her bed. And if she shuts you out in the kitchen, yowl until morning."

The Mean Monstrosity nodded slowly. "OK, Mr. D," he said. "But this better work, see? Or you're *history*."

That was Sunday. Now all we had to do was wait.

Luckily for The Mean Monstrosity, it rained last night. By then, Number 13 had lost a take-out order of fish and chips and Number 14 had lost five squid. Now, there are only fourteen houses in our street, and if my theory was right, Numbers 1 and 2 would never lose anything at all. Sylvester Slink (if it *was* Sylvester Slink) would never steal from his own house, and he wouldn't take anything from The Mean Monstrosity's either, because that would blow his cover. So, if I was right, it was time for the cat burglar to hit my house again, Number 3.

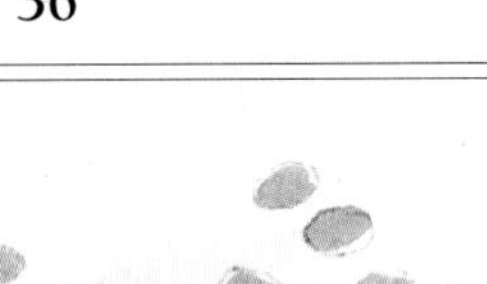

MRD

When I saw the rain clouds, I couldn't believe my luck. First, I dragged a leg of lamb out of the fridge and propped it near the dog flap. Then I had a huge supper. Then I pretended to go to sleep under the table.

Hours passed.

I heard the rain begin.

I saw the lights go out in Number 2.

I heard The Mean Monstrosity begin to yowl.

I waited.

The trouble with pretending to be asleep is that sometimes you *do* go to sleep. Especially if you've had a huge supper. I woke up to see a watery sort of daylight and no leg of lamb. The cat burglar had struck again!

"Woo-woo-woof!" I barked. "Woo-woo-*woof*!" That fetched The Family out at once.

My Missus looked at the greasy marks on the floor. She opened the fridge. "Oh *no*!" she said, and stormed off next door to Number 2.

Sylvester Slink was outside, washing his shoulder blades on the path.

"Hi!" I said. "Heard the latest?"

Sylvester Slink spat out some hair.

"The cat burglar's *really* done it this time," I said. "He's stolen a whole leg of lamb!"

"Really?" said Sylvester Slink dreamily. "*I* heard it was only a lamb bone with chewed edges."

"Now I wonder where you heard that?" I said.

He licked his whiskers nervously. "Around."

"Sylvester Slink," I said, "I accuse *you* of being the cat burglar of Pethaven Drive."

"Oh come *on*," scoffed Sylvester Slink. "Everyone knows it's The Mean Monstrosity."

"Not this time," I said. "This time *I've* got proof and *he's* got a cast-iron alibi."

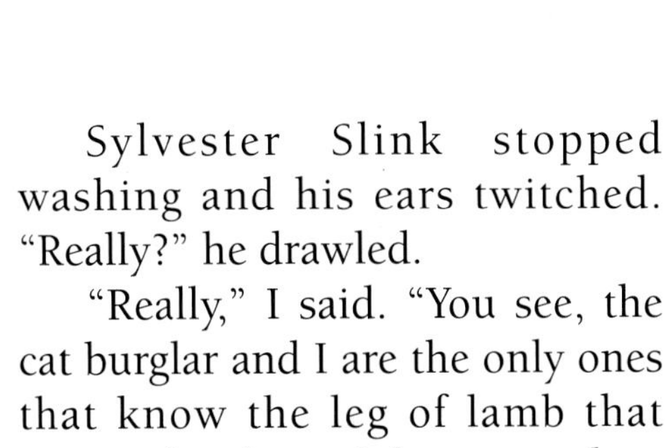

Sylvester Slink stopped washing and his ears twitched. “Really?” he drawled.

“Really,” I said. “You see, the cat burglar and I are the only ones that know the leg of lamb that was stolen last night was only a bone. That’s my proof. As for The Mean Monstrosity’s alibi; I take it you didn’t know he never, *never* goes out in the rain?”

Sylvester Slink nodded two or three times. “Thank you for that information,” he said. “Pity you didn’t tell me before.” And he slid away.

That’s just about the end of the story. The Mean Monstrosity’s Missus told my Missus The Mean Monstrosity had been yowling in *her* kitchen all night, so he couldn’t have been in our kitchen stealing legs of lamb.

My Missus told all the neighbors.

That let The Mean Monstrosity off the hook.

There was no way I could tell The Family the real identity of the cat burglar of Pethaven Drive, but I didn't care. I knew Sylvester Slink wouldn't steal if he didn't have someone else to take the rap.

And as for The Mean Monstrosity, he's been almost friendly today. Except twice when he forgot himself and spat in my eye. Then we had a good old chase for old times' sake.

And Sylvester Slink? I must say he's a cool customer. This evening he was back outside my door, washing his ears with his paws. He didn't say anything, but I could tell from the look in his eyes that one day he's going to get his revenge. I'm quite glad, really. It gives me something to look forward to.

And that is the end of the story. So, if you'll excuse me, I'll just lie back and sleep off that enormous supper I had last night. All the meat from a leg of lamb.

Well, *someone* had to eat it.

TITLES IN THE SERIES

SET 9A

Television Drama
Time for Sale
The Shady Deal
The Loch Ness Monster Mystery
Secrets of the Desert

SET 9B

To JJ From CC
Pandora's Box
The Birthday Disaster
The Song of the Mantis
Helping the Hoiho

SET 9C

Glumly
Rupert and the Griffin
The Tree, the Trunk, and the Tuba
Errol the Peril
Cassidy's Magic

SET 9D

Barney
Get a Grip, Pip!
Casey's Case
Dear Future
Strange Meetings

SET 10A

A Battle of Words
The Rainbow Solution
Fortune's Friend
Eureka
It's a Frog's Life

SET 10B

The Cat Burglar of Pethaven Drive
The Matchbox
In Search of the Great Bears
Many Happy Returns
Spider Relatives

SET 10C

Horrible Hank
Brian's Brilliant Career
Fernitickles
It's All in Your Mind, James Robert
Wing High, Gooftah

SET 10D

The Week of the Jellyhoppers
Timothy Whuffenpuffen-Whippersnapper
Timedetectors
Ryan's Dog Ringo
The Secret of Kiribu Tapu Lagoon